# GEORGE

*George Washington, Our Founding Father*

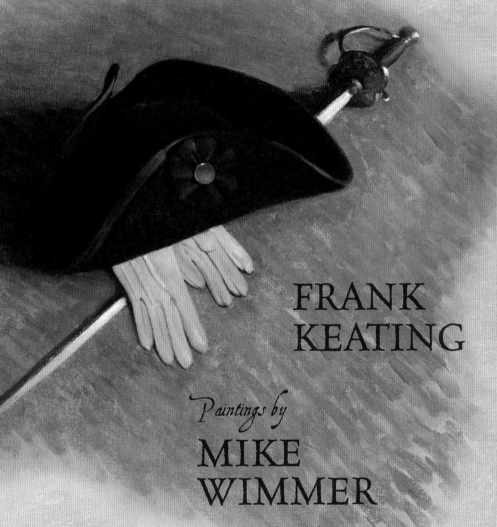

FRANK
KEATING

*Paintings by*
MIKE
WIMMER

*A Paula Wiseman Book*
Simon & Schuster Books for Young Readers
NEW YORK  LONDON  TORONTO  SYDNEY  NEW DELHI

The author, illustrator, and publisher gratefully acknowledge the
Mount Vernon Ladies' Association for their help in creating this book.

SIMON & SCHUSTER BOOKS FOR YOUNG READERS • An imprint of Simon & Schuster Children's Publishing Division •
1230 Avenue of the Americas, New York, New York 10020 • Text copyright © 2012 by Frank Keating • Illustrations copyright © 2012
by Mike Wimmer • All rights reserved, including the right of reproduction in whole or in part in any form. • SIMON & SCHUSTER
BOOKS FOR YOUNG READERS is a trademark of Simon & Schuster, Inc. • For information about special discounts for bulk purchases,
please contact Simon & Schuster Special Sales at 1-866-506-1949 or business@simonandschuster.com. • The Simon & Schuster
Speakers Bureau can bring authors to your live event. • For more information or to book an event, contact the Simon & Schuster
Speakers Bureau at 1-866-248-3049 or visit our website at www.simonspeakers.com. • Book design by Chloë Foglia • The text for this
book is set in Celestia Antiqua Std. • The illustrations for this book are rendered in oil on canvas. • Manufactured in China • 1011 SCP
2 4 6 8 10 9 7 5 3 1
Library of Congress Cataloging-in-Publication Data • Keating, Francis Anthony, 1944– • George : George Washington, our founding
father / Frank Keating ; illustrated by Mike Wimmer. • p. cm. • Summary: "The fifth of ten children, George Washington was a
dreamer, a hard worker, an athlete, and a peacemaker. By the time he was fifteen he had handwritten for himself the "Rules of
Civility and Decent Behavior in Company and Conversation." These were his rules to live by. He could not have known what his
future would hold . . . and these rules speak to who he was as a boy and a man. Based on this little known historical document,
this is George Washington's life from boyhood to his presidency"—Provided by publisher. • Includes bibliographical references.
• ISBN 978-1-4169-5482-8 (hardback) • 1. Washington, George, 1732-1799—Juvenile literature. 2. Presidents—United States—
Biography—Juvenile literature. I. Wimmer, Mike, ill. II. Title. III. Title: George Washington, our founding father. E312.66.K43
2012 • 973.4 1092—dc23 • [B] • 2011013322 • ISBN 978-1-4424-4717-2 (eBook)

Editor's Note: All quotations are the words of George Washington. Archaic spelling, capitalization,
and punctuation in historical quotations have been modernized throughout the text.

My special grandchildren, Catie, Will, Matthew, Hadley, Emma, Chloe, Callie, Mary Frances, and Frank, are young Americans who will soon learn of the luster and legacy of our nation's first president. This book is dedicated to them. But it is also dedicated to the regents, vice regents, and staff of Mount Vernon, without whose professionalism and devotion to Washington's memory, the light of the nation's father would be considerably dimmed.

*— F. K.*

For Paula Wiseman, whose guidance and friendship have given me a voice with which I can speak to the ages

*— M. W.*

*I* am remembered as the Father of My Country.

The indispensable man.

First in War.

First in Peace.

First in the hearts of my countrymen.

———◆■◆———

Rule 110:

*Labor to keep alive in your breast that little spark of celestial fire called conscience.*

———◆■◆———

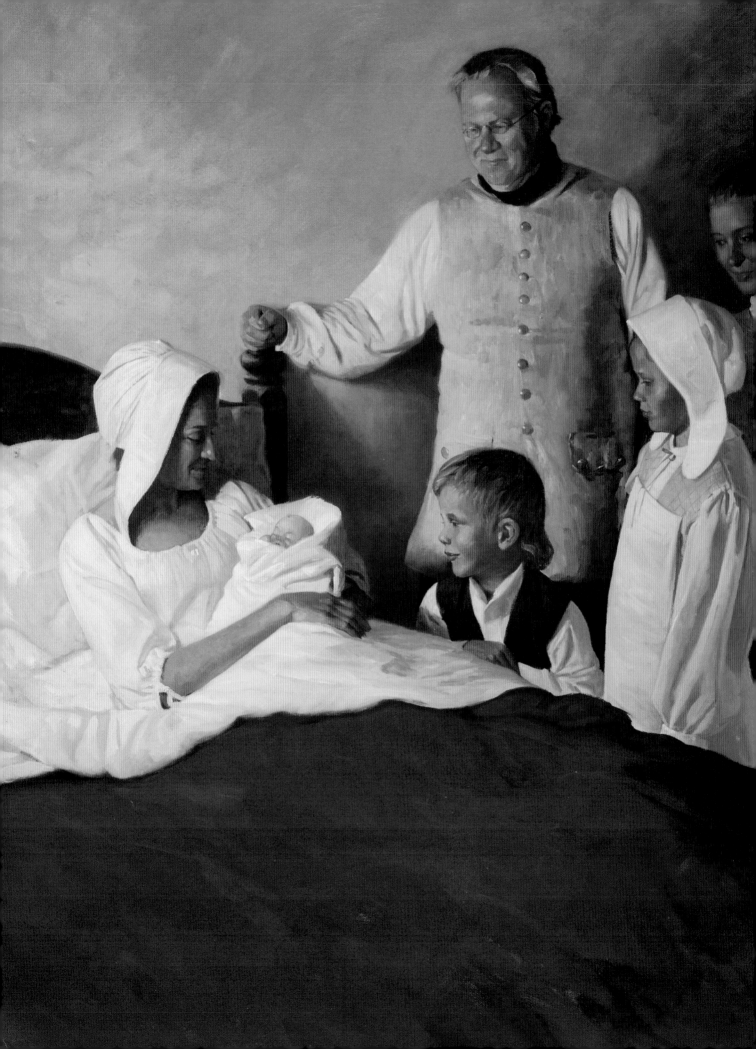

First I was a child.

I was born February 22, 1732, the fifth of ten children. My Virginia birthplace was a house built on a bed of oyster shells. My parents were Augustine and Mary Ball Washington. To my great sadness, my father died when I was eleven.

In school I studied hard. Arithmetic. Penmanship. Reading. I began to write a list of rules that my teachers taught me. Rules of character that I knew I must always remember.

At play I was tall and strong. Frequently I was asked to be the peacemaker. I formed a company of boy soldiers at school. I was chosen captain and spent hours of fun marching my friends across the grass.

◆■◆

Rule 73:

*Think before you speak. Pronounce not imperfectly nor bring out your words too hastily, but orderly and distinctly.*

◆■◆

When my classmates and I had no books to read, we entertained ourselves by memorizing the names and verses from old tombstones.

Some were quite funny:

"John Hizer,

The Mizer,

Is wiser—we hope."

---

Rule 74:

*When another speaks, be attentive yourself and disturb not the audience. If any hesitate in his words, help him not nor prompt him without desired, interrupt him not, nor answer him till his speech be ended.*

At age fifteen my formal education ended. Though "defective" to my mind, it was not unusual for children of my time to finish school at a young age. Since my father had passed away, I was expected to help my mother care for our large family.

Rule 56:

*Associate yourself with men of good quality if you esteem your own reputation, for 'tis better to be alone than in bad company.*

When I left school, I became a surveyor. I was also a blacksmith and a carpenter. I could make a barrel about as well as a cooper could. My work became a classroom of life lessons. I learned from experience.

I grew by reading and observing. Good manners bred good morals. And good morals produced a respected and successful adult. I applied the "Rules of Civility" to all that I did. I put them to practice. They were my primer on life. I first learned them in school. I wrote them down. They became a part of me.

◄•■•►

Rule 82:

*Undertake not what you cannot perform but be careful to keep your promise.*

◄•■•►

In my twenties I was in the midst of the action.
I was a major of militia. I was "bent to arms," and
volunteered to lead a party through nine hundred
miles of wilderness to deliver a message to the French.
I was young, but I was trusted.

———◆■◆———

Rule 35:

*Let your discourse with men of business be short and comprehensive.*

———◆■◆———

I was trained and confident. I was selected to lead. The weather was bone-chilling. I parleyed with Indians. A bullet fired "not fifteen steps" away nearly struck me. I was thrown into a swift roaring river and almost drowned. But my strength and will to survive saved me. For months I withstood cold and hardship, yet I accomplished my mission and came home a respected and wiser man.

Rule 1:
*Every action done in company ought to be with some sign of respect to those that are present.*

Later I returned to the woods and accompanied our English forces on a mission to eject the French from their claims to the Ohio Valley. The battle was the opening of a worldwide seven-year war that would drive the French from North America and place our British cousins firmly in charge of the continent. "I heard the bullets whistle," I wrote. Four bullet holes were in my coat and two horses were wounded under me. A lead ball passed through my hat. Our effort was unsuccessful, but I had done my boldest and best. I came home a hero.

At age twenty-seven I married Martha, a widow and mother of two children, Patsy and Jacky. I had no children of my own.

My principles were clear. The lesson plan was straightforward. The Rules of Civility had been a part of me since I copied them when I was fifteen. They sustained me through the birth of our nation.

When Virginia and the other colonies began the great debate for independence, I was there.

I wore my uniform to the sessions of Congress. I was unanimously selected as commander in chief of our armies. I devoted myself solely to "American union and patriotism."

———◆■◆———

Rule 44:

*When a man does all he can, though it succeeds not well, blame not him that did it.*

———◆■◆———

I remembered the advice of my youth.

I kept my promise. I was the first soldier commissioned by my country. I remained in the army and did not return home until each battle was won.

Darkness and defeat. Success and uncertainty. But never despair. The virtue of my men and the nobility of our cause would ultimately bring our reward.

God was an active agent in all that we were attempting.

◄•■•►

Rule 108:

*When you speak of God or His attributes, let it be seriously and with reverence.*

◄•■•►

Our prayers were answered. This "wonderful Revolution" was won, and those who would treat us as slaves were forced from our shores.

But the ending was just the beginning. The new nation was weak.

We had national "character" to establish. The country needed to defend liberty and provide for representative government. "The preservation of the sacred fire of liberty and the destiny of the republican model of government" were staked on this experiment. A constitutional convention was called. I was unanimously chosen as its president. We began our task.

Finally our work was done. The Constitution, few in words, created a national government while limiting the powers of that government. It was a document devoted to the common good.

When the states accepted the Constitution, I was unanimously elected as our country's first president, and then elected again for a second term.

I led a great people. To make a great land.

To create a better world.

George Washington, our founding father, led us to independence in the Revolutionary War and was the first president of our nation. He was born in 1732, and though no photographs of him exist, one way we can understand him is through the "Rules of Civility" he copied as a young schoolboy with the help of his teachers in Virginia. These are rules that George Washington compiled to guide his life. For a complete list of the rules, visit gwpapers.virginia.edu.

As a young boy, George Washington couldn't have known he would become the first president of a new country, but the seeds of leadership and greatness were planted in his early years. It is my hope that by my sharing some of the incidents of young George Washington's life, made all the more real by Mike Wimmer's glowing paintings, you will have a better understanding of who George Washington was and how his life was shaped to influence our country and our lives so many years later.

The paintings for this book were created using oil paints on canvas. I first generated a number of sketches to create interesting compositions to bring the viewer into the story, as if we were a direct witness to the events that molded the character of America's first president, George Washington. I did this by employing models to portray the characters. I then chose the correct lighting that would best amplify the quiet drama of each moment. Then I created completely finished sketches before I transferred the image to canvas. My under painting was usually done in a monochromatic value that best reflected the mood of the scene. I then finished the painting, concentrating on the focal point of the narrative, utilizing contrast of color, value, or brushwork.

Each painting was meticulously researched for costume accuracy and setting. Paintings of the period were an enormous help. I engrossed myself with the details of George's life, and he became more real to me. This allowed me to better portray him as a human being rather than the iconic figure he has become through myth and legend.

I want to thank a few of the people and organizations that helped me bring this project to fruition. James C. Rees, executive director of Mount Vernon, and the regents and staff allowed me unfettered access to the grounds and artifacts that enabled me to reproduce with such accuracy. Thanks also to the dedicated group of re-enactors at the Fort Loudoun State Historic Area in Vonore, Tennessee. Whit Edwards and other re-enactors of the Oklahoma History Center were invaluable in bringing to life the period of the revolution.

It was indeed a challenge and an honor to bring to life this heroic character. I want each of the readers to come away with a deep respect for this common man, who made uncommon choices that positioned our small country for the greatness that we today are the recipients of.

---

## Historic Notes on the Art Rendered in This Book

Page 4: Washington in uniform during the Revolutionary War.

Page 8: Washington attended Henry Williams School and had minimal formal education.

Page 14: Washington interned under surveyor George Fairfax.

Page 18: Washington traveled the Ohio Valley and encountered many tribes during the French and Indian War.

Pages 20–21: This scene of 1755 represents fighting during the French and Indian War, in which British general Edward Braddock was killed in Pennsylvania.

Page 24: A session of the Second Continental Congress, which was held from 1775 to 1781.

Page 26: Washington at Valley Forge during the winter of 1777.

Page 28: A scene from the Battle of Yorktown in 1781.

Page 30: Washington on the portico of Mount Vernon looking out over the Potomac.

## Bibliography

Brookhiser, Richard. *Founding Father: Rediscovering George Washington.* New York: Free Press, 1997.

Burns, James MacGregor, and Susan Dunn. *George Washington.* New York: Times Books, 2004.

Clark, Harrison. *All Cloudless Glory, Volume One.* New York: Regnery Publishing, 1998.

d'Aulaire, Ingri, and Edgar Parin d'Aulaire. *George Washington.* San Luis Obispo, CA: Beautiful Feet Books, 1996. First published 1936 by Doubleday, Doran.

Flexner, James Thomas. *George Washington.* Boston: Little, Brown, 1965.

Stevenson, Augusta. *George Washington, Our First Leader.* New York: Aladdin Books, 1988.

Warren, Jack D., Jr. *Northern Neck of Virginia Historical Magazine.* December 1999.

Washington, George. *The Journal of Major George Washington.* Williamsburg, VA: Colonial Williamsburg Foundation, 1754.